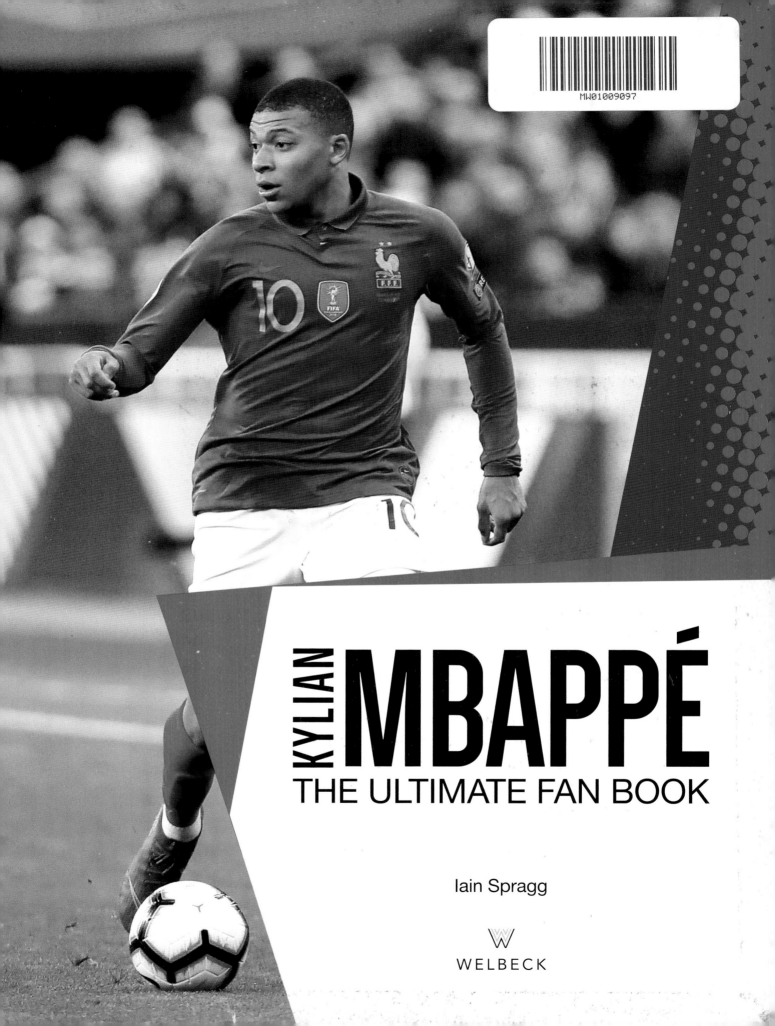

KYLIAN MBAPPÉ
THE ULTIMATE FAN BOOK

Iain Spragg

WELBECK

CONTENTS

Mbappé has emerged as one of the hottest talents in world football since his record-breaking transfer to PSG in 2017.

INTRODUCTION

Football's hottest young talent, Kylian Mbappé has rewritten the record books for at both club and country levels since making his professional debut at the age of 16.

The striker only turned 21 at the end of 2019 but the youngster has already achieved more than most professional players do in their entire careers, winning the FIFA World Cup and three French league titles with Monaco and Paris Saint-Germain.

This book is the incredible story of the boy from the poor suburb of Bondy in Paris and how he has risen rapidly through the football ranks to become a world champion and one of the hottest talents on the planet.

Mbappé's remarkable journey has seen the star shine for Monaco as a teenager before heading back to the bright lights of Paris, amazing the PSG crowds in the French capital with his explosive pace, vision and jaw-dropping tricks.

At international level, the striker was just 18 when he made his France debut but little over a year later he was starring for *Les Bleus* in the FIFA World Cup final, scoring a brilliant goal in the 4-2 win over Croatia in Moscow to become only the third teenager to lift the famous trophy.

His brilliant displays for PSG and France have also brought Mbappé a huge haul of individual awards and in the last two seasons he has been crowned the French Player of the Year, Ligue 1 Player of the Year and the FIFA World Cup Best Young Player.

Kylian Mbappé:The Ultimate Fan Book is a celebration of the French genius, a true superstar who looks destined to become the greatest player in world football.

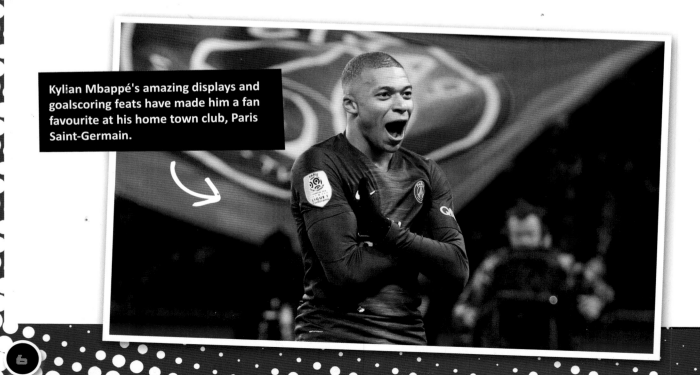

Kylian Mbappé's amazing displays and goalscoring feats have made him a fan favourite at his home town club, Paris Saint-Germain.

The French star was just 19 years old when he helped his country lift the World Cup in 2018 in Russia.

THE EARLY YEARS

Kylian Mbappé grew up in a tough area of the French capital Paris, surrounded by posters of his hero Cristiano Ronaldo on his bedroom walls.

Mbappé was born in Paris on December 23, 1998. It was just over five months after France had famously won the FIFA World Cup for the first time, beating Brazil in the final at the Stade de France, less than 10 kilometres from the Mbappé family home in the north east of the city.

His father Wilfried was a refugee from Cameroon while his mother Fayza was a French-Algerian. He has an adopted brother, Jirès Kembo Ekoko, who is 10 years older than him, while his younger brother Ethan was born in 2006.

Things were not easy for the family in suburb of Bondy and it got worse in autumn 2005 – when Mbappé was just six years old – because the area was affected by riots as local youngsters fought with police.

The young Mbappé, however, had only football on his mind. A year earlier he had joined his local club, AS Bondy and, even then, was determined to fulfil his dream of becoming a professional footballer.

"I have had a career plan since my youngest age," he said. "I know what I want to do, where I want to go and I will not let anything disturb me."

His football hero was Cristiano Ronaldo. The Portuguese superstar was a Manchester United player when Mbappé joined AS Bondy in 2004, and his bedroom was covered with posters of the Old Trafford legend. Little did he know that eight years later he would get the chance to meet his idol, now playing for Real Madrid, in person.

Mbappé made a big impression at AS Bondy and it was soon obvious he had huge potential. "He had technique and vision in the game that most children just don't have," said club president Atmane Airouche. "He never played for his proper age group, he always played with older children because there was no point leaving him with kids his own age."

Growing up in his home city of Paris, the teenage Mbappé worshipped Portugal legend Cristiano Ronaldo.

Mbappé's amazing football journey began when he joined local club AS Bondy at the age of five.

A SPORTING FAMILY

The speed of Mbappé's spectacular rise up the football ranks came as no surprise those who knew his family and their proud sporting background.

Few players can reach the top of the professional game without parental support and Mbappé was lucky to have a father and mother who both played a huge part in him becoming one of the football's biggest stars.

His dad Wilfried was a talented amateur player who became a coach at AS Bondy in 1993, and coached his young son even before he joined AS Bondy. Wilfried is now Kylian's agent. His mum was a professional handball player in France before he was born and taught him the discipline needed to make it to the top.

"He was born into football and sport," said Atmane Airouche, the president of AS Bondy. "His father was a youth leader, working with children in the local area and then he was brought in to AS Bondy.

"His imprint will be here forever. He gave 25 years of his life to us. And his mother is also a big influence. She was a very good professional handball player.

"You could say that Kylian was born here at this club. He was here when his father was a player and a coach. He was always here and learning about football."

The family influence didn't stop there. His older, adopted brother Jirès Kembo Ekoko was also a footballer and in 2006, when Mbappé was seven

Mbappe's parents were a big influence on the youngster as he pursued his dream of becoming a professional footballer.

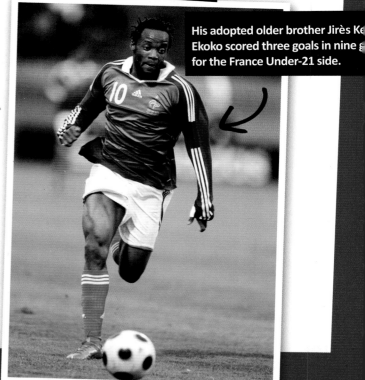

His adopted older brother Jirès Ke Ekoko scored three goals in nine g for the France Under-21 side.

years old, he turned professional with French first division club Rennes. Ekoko – whose biological father played for Zaire in the 1974 FIFA World Cup – earned France Under-21 international honours and spent six seasons with the club before going to play in Abu Dhabi, Dubai and Turkey.

Kylian also has a younger brother, Ethan. Born in 2006, he is already part of the PSG youth set-up and looks set to follow his brother into the professional ranks. In April 2019, Ethan was invited to join the famous French FA football academy in Clairefontaine.

Mbappé's younger brother Ethan is already a PSG youth player and tipped to follow in his sibling's footsteps.

AN ENGLISH ADVENTURE

Even before he became a teenager, Mbappé was being chased by Europe's biggest clubs and, in 2010, he crossed the English Channel for a trial at Chelsea.

Mbappé was still a few months short of his 12th birthday when Chelsea's French scout, Guy Hillion, invited him and his family for a week-long visit to London. The reigning Premier League champions had heard all about the youngster from Paris and were eager to see him in action.

The 11-year-old was taken on a tour of Stamford Bridge, meeting first-team manager Carlo Ancelotti and star striker Didier Drogba. He also played for the club's Under-12 side in a friendly against Charlton Athletic. The Blues youngsters won the match 8-0.

"It was a wonderful experience," he said later. "Chelsea was the first great club, the first big club, that I went to visit. So it was a real discovery for me. I was coming from my grassroots, amateur club. It was a whole new world.

"Of course I had an idea what a great football club was like, but I was really impressed by the working culture and the mentality of wanting to be better day in, day out. Visiting this infrastructure helped me with my development. I always thought, 'I want to be there, I want to be one of those big players who is trying to give people fun out of the game'."

His parents however didn't want to their young son to move to England and, six months later, despite interest from other big clubs like Manchester City, Manchester United, Bayern Munich and Liverpool, he joined the French FA's academy in Clairefontaine.

Two years later, the family were invited to Spain by Real Madrid and although the 13-year-old met his football hero Cristiano Ronaldo, as well as club legend Zinedine Zidane, the Mbappés were determined that Kylian would he start his professional career back home in France.

"We did not go to Madrid to learn more about our son's potential," Wilfried said, "but to please him."

Italian Carlo Ancelotti was the Chelsea boss when Mbappé was invited to Stamford Bridge for a trial in 2010.

As a young player, Mbappé trained regularly at the famous French football academy in Clairefontaine.

Mbappé renewed acquaintances with Chelsea legend Didier Drogba at the UNFP awards ceremony in May 2019.

TURNING PROFESSIONAL

At the age of 14, Mbappé agreed to join French Ligue 1 club AS Monaco, making his record-breaking senior debut for the club just three years later.

A player's first professional contract can sometimes make or break a career. Many young footballers make the mistake of signing for a big club and never make it to the first team. Mbappé's parents were determined he wouldn't fall into that trap.

It was for this reason, in 2012, that they decided Monaco was the perfect place for Kylian. The club might have been over 400 miles from the family home in Paris but it was where they believed the 13-year-old had the best chance of developing his talent and becoming a world-class player.

"This is the club that has helped me grow," he said in an interview in 2016. "I feel good here, and I'm going to be able to continue taking new steps forward."

Monaco had no doubt they had a potential superstar on their hands. "When I first heard about him my colleagues said 'Look, we have a very talented boy, we have to sign him'," said club vice-president Vadim Vasilyev. "So I said 'What's the problem? Let's sign him. I knew that he was a phenomenon. It's not just "very good", it's not "top", it is a phenomenal player'."

His early years in the principality saw Mbappé working his way through the Monaco youth ranks. At every stage he impressed the club's coaches with his maturity and skill and it wasn't long before the first team manager Leonardo Jardim decided he was ready for his senior debut.

It came in December 2015 in a Ligue 1 clash with Caen at the Stade Louis II. Mbappé started the match on the bench but he got the call from Jardim and, with 88 minutes on the clock, he replaced Portuguese international defender Fábio Coentrão.

At the age of just 16 years and 347 days, Mbappé became the youngest debutant in Monaco's history, breaking the record previously set by the legendary striker Thierry Henry 21 years earlier.

The picturesque setting of Monaco's Stade Louis II stadium.

Mbappé impressed coaches at every age level at Monaco. It was clear he would not have to wait long for a first team debut.

TEENAGE KICKS

Following his first team debut, Mbappé enhanced his growing reputation with a series of dazzling performances for the Red and Whites.

The teenager may have had little time to impress in his first senior appearance against Caen but manager Leonardo Jardim was convinced the teenager was the real deal and, eight days later, named him on the bench for Monaco's UEFA Europa League Group J clash with Tottenham Hotspur in London in December 2015.

Mbappé was called into action in the 56th minute at White Hart Lane and after another substitute appearance in Ligue 1 against Saint-Étienne, he was named in the starting XI for the first time. It was a League Cup fixture against Bordeaux, and Kylian played the full 90 minutes.

The best however was yet to come and, in February 2016, he rewrote the Monaco record books when he came off the bench to score his first senior goal against Troyes, sprinting into the box in injury time and finishing stylishly with his left foot.

His goal completed a 3-1 win for the club but, more significantly, it made him Monaco's youngest ever scorer at the age of 17 years and 63 days.

"Mbappé secured a place in the record books on Saturday by becoming the youngest goal scorer in Monaco's history – displacing Thierry Henry in the process," reported the BBC Sport website. "He will be all right if he goes on to have a career anywhere near as good as that of Henry, who was 17 years and 254 days when he struck his first goal for the club against Lens in April 1995. Henry went on to

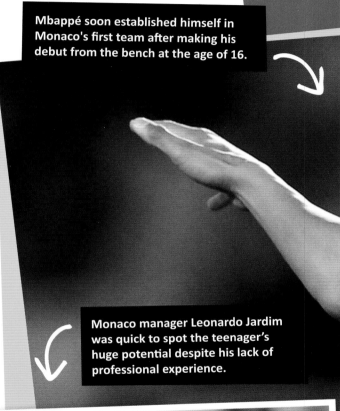

Mbappé soon established himself in Monaco's first team after making his debut from the bench at the age of 16.

Monaco manager Leonardo Jardim was quick to spot the teenager's huge potential despite his lack of professional experience.

win the World Cup with France in 1998. Not that Mbappe is old enough to remember."

The teenager made six more Ligue 1 appearances for the club in the 2015–16 season. Two came in the starting line-up and four from the bench as Monaco finished third and although he didn't find the back of the net again, Mbappé was rapidly making a name for himself as one of hottest young talents in France.

His first taste of European football came against Tottenham at White Hart Lane in Monaco's 2015–16 Europa League campaign.

EUROPEAN CHAMPION

After breaking into Monaco's first team Mbappé headed to Germany in the summer of 2016 to represent his country in the UEFA European Under-19 Championship.

France's bid to be crowned European champions for the first time in six years began with a disappointing 2-1 defeat to England in the group stage, but thanks to a brilliant three-match scoring streak from Mbappé, it was *Les Bleus* who lifted the trophy at the end of the tournament.

His first goal came three days after the England loss, in a 2-0 victory over Croatia in Aalen, and Mbappé was on target again in the final group game, against the Netherlands, grabbing a brace in

Mbappé's selection for France's UEFA European Under-19 Championship squad underlined the teenager's rapid rise up the ranks.

a thumping 5-1 win against the Dutch.

France qualified for the semi-finals, where they played Portugal. The match was level at 1-1 at half-time but Mbappé was the real star of the show after the break, netting in the 67th and 75th minutes to seal a 3-1 victory and send the French team into the final.

Italy stood between France and the silverware and although he wasn't one of *Les Bleus'* scorers in their 4-0 win at Stuttgart's Rhein-Neckar-Arena in front of a crowd of 25,000, Mbappé terrorized the Italian defence from start to finish.

The tournament confirmed him as one of European football's brightest talents. His tally of five goals made him the second-top scorer in Germany, just one behind team-mate Jean-Kévin Augustin. He was also named in the UEFA Team of the Tournament but the teenager refused to let success go to his head.

"We went to watch him in the final," said Atmane Airouche, president of his old club AS Bondy. "We met him outside the stadium and we were shocked that he didn't go out partying with his team-mates. Instead he wanted to go straight home. To him he had achieved his goal to be European champion and was already thinking about his next goal – going back to Monaco, getting into the team and winning more titles."

Mbappé scored twice in the second-half in the semi-final against Portugal to book France's place in the final.

Les Bleus thumping 4-0 win in the final against Italy saw France crowned Under-19 European champions for the eighth time.

WINNING THE LEAGUE

In only his second season of senior football, Mbappé was in sensational form in front of goal as Monaco were crowned French champions for the first time in 17 years.

Mbappé was aged just 17 when the 2016–17 season started. His reputation was already growing, and his performances didn't disappoint. Monaco charged to the Ligue 1 title, eight points clear of second-place Paris Saint-Germain.

He opened the season in the Leonardo Jardim's starting line-up and, in October, he opened his goal-scoring account with one in a 6-2 demolition of Montpellier.

Two weeks later he was on target again against Nancy but the best was yet to come. In February, Mbappé struck the first league hat-trick of his career in a 5-0 thrashing of Metz. This treble made him the youngest player to grab a Ligue 1 hat-trick for 12 years.

In March, he netted a double against Nantes, which took his tally in the league to 10. In the process Mbappé became the youngest player to reach double figures in Ligue 1 for 30 years. Later the same month, his dazzling form saw him called into the France squad for the first time. On March 25, 2017, in a World Cup qualifier against Luxembourg, Mbappé came off the bench after 78 minutes to replace Dimitri Payet and make his international debut.

The goals kept flowing as did his reputation. In April he was named Player of the Month and, in May, he a scored his 15th Ligue 1 goal in a 2-0 victory over Saint-Etienne. This win confirmed Monaco as champions.

"We've been able to hold on all the way against teams like Paris and Nice who kept up with the pace until the end," Mbappé said. "Unfortunately for them, but luckily for us, we're the ones leaving with the trophy."

It had been a stunning breakthrough season for Mbappé and individual awards quickly followed. He was voted the Ligue 1 Young Player of the Year and was named in the Ligue 1 Team of the Year. In December 2017, the month he turned 19, he was named France's Young Player of the Year, completing an incredible year for the outrageously talented teenager.

The forward netted 15 league goals in 29 appearances in 2016 to fire Monaco to the Ligue 1 title.

Mbappé's brilliant breakthrough season was recognized when he was named the Ligue 1 Young Player of the Year.

STORMING THE EUROPEAN STAGE

Mbappé was the breakout star of the UEFA Champions League in 2016–17, top scoring for Monaco as the French champions fought their way through to the semi-finals.

The Champions League is the biggest club competition in European football and Mbappé made a real name for himself in 2016–17 as Monaco defied the odds to reach the last four, knocking out heavyweights Manchester City and Borussia Dortmund along the way.

The teenager's debut in the tournament came in late September in the group stage against German side Bayer Leverkusen. Home and away appearances against CSKA Moscow followed and in February he bagged his first Champions League goal in the first leg of his team's round of 16 clash

Mbappé was the driving force behind Monaco's surprise march into the Champions League semi-finals.

The teenager made his Champions League debut against Bayer Leverkusen in September 2016.

against Manchester City.

Monaco were beaten 5-3 in England but Mbappé inspired an incredible fightback in the return leg at the Stade Louis II, scoring an eighth-minute goal to set up a thrilling 3-1 win which sent the French side through on the away goals rule.

Dortmund were Monaco's quarter-final opponents and Mbappé proved the difference between the two sides with a double in the away leg in Germany and another goal in a 3-1 triumph at home seven days later.

It was the first time Monaco had reached the last four of the Champions League for 13 years and although Italian giants Juventus were too strong for them in the semi-final, going through 4-1 on aggregate, Mbappé made further headlines with yet another goal against the Serie A champions in Turin.

His six goals in 2016–17 were more than other Monaco player in the tournament and also made him the joint most prolific Frenchman in the competition alongside Atletico Madrid's Antoine Greizmann. Mbappé had taken his place alongside's European elite.

In recognition of his performances, UEFA named him as one of 18 players in its Champions League Team of the Season which included his boyhood idol Cristiano Ronaldo, as well as superstars Lionel Messi, Sergio Ramos and Toni Kroos.

In November 2017, after 26 goals in 44 games in 2016–17, he was named the European Young Player of the Year to underline his amazing rise from youth team hopeful to world-class star.

He scored home and away against Premier League giants Manchester City in the last 16 to secure Monaco's place in the quarter-finals.

AT HOME WITH MBAPPÉ

When he's not tormenting defences on the pitch, the young Frenchman has a surprisingly simple life in his hometown of Paris.

Mbappé may have found fame and fortune at a young age but despite his incredible success he remains a modest and generous person who does not like to show off his wealth or live a celebrity lifestyle like other footballers.

"I may be ahead of my age, but in real life I am still a kid," he said in an interview in 2018. "Footballer does not rhyme with Ferrari. I have no car, it's not a big deal."

He showed his generosity during the 2018 World Cup finals when he decided to donate his match fees to charity. Mbappé earned £18,000 for each match appearance in Russia, plus a £270,000 bonus for winning the tournament.

Rather than banking the cash he gave it to Premiers de Cordée, a charity which organizes sporting events for children with disabilities.

"I earn enough money, a lot of money," he said. "I think it is important to help those who are in need. A lot of people are suffering, a lot of people have diseases. For people like us, giving a helping hand to people is not a big thing.

"It doesn't change my life, but it changes theirs. And if it can change theirs, it is a great pleasure. I gave the money to the charity where I am a sponsor because being handicapped is something difficult. Showing them that they can do sports like everyone it is something close to my heart."

When Mbappé isn't playing football, his favourite sport is tennis. His favourite player is fellow Frenchman Jo-Wilfried Tsonga, while he met legend Roger Federer at the 2019 French Open, presenting the Swiss star with a France shirt.

Mbappé has been a big fan of trainers since he was young. "I like to have my small collection," he said. "It always feels good to rock an old pair from time to time. I'm like a kid with a new toy when I get a new pair of sneakers. I've always been a sneaker lover so it's a pleasure to buy new pairs and mix them with my clothes to flex a little."

Mbappé is a big tennis fan and was in the crowd at the French Open in 2019 to watch Roger Federer.

Mbappé showed his charitable side when he donated his 2018 World Cup match fees to local charity Premiers de Cordée.

SUPER SKILLS

Mbappé boasts all the technical and physical attributes to make him one of the best players on the planet.

The PSG star's natural movement on the pitch is one of his trademarks and makes him almost impossible to mark.

OFF THE BALL
Mbappé's instinctive movement off the ball is a trademark of his game. He is one of the best in the world in finding space when a team-mate has the ball and he's superb in ghosting into the penalty area to get on the end of crosses.

THROUGH THE MIDDLE
Often deployed out wide, Mbappé is just as dangerous playing through the middle when required. His pace, movement and hunger for goals make him a nightmare for central defenders.

WIDE MAN
Although naturally right-footed, Mbappé is devastating on either flank. Playing on the right, he can cut in and use his "weaker" left foot or operate wide left, opening up space by coming in onto his stronger foot.

DEADLY DRIBBLING
Speed is nothing without control and Mbappé's ability to keep the ball at his feet while sprinting is incredible. It often seems like the ball is tied to him on a piece of string even when he is in full stride.

Like all genuinely world-class attacking players, Mbappé is brilliant in the air and deadly with his head.

HEAD BOY

Although he is 1.78m (5ft 10in) tall, Mbappé is a real aerial threat. He can rise above taller, bigger defenders with brilliantly-timed leaps, giving him the time and space to score from close range with his head.

NEED FOR SPEED

Raw pace is one of Mbappé's main attacking weapons and when he is in full flow, he terrorizes opposition defences with his incredible turn of speed. Few players in the world can live with his amazing acceleration and natural ability to twist inside or out.

There are few players on the planet who can keep up with the French superstar when he is in full flow.

GREAT MONACO GOALS

The French star scored some stunning goals in his two seasons with the Ligue 1 club. These are five of his best.

MANCHESTER CITY 5 **MONACO 3**
Champions League, February 21, 2017
Mbappé scored his first Champions League goal in spectacular style with a thunderbolt against City at the Etihad. He was quickest to react to a looping through ball into the City area and unleashed an unstoppable half-volley that screamed past Willy Caballero's gloves into the roof of the net.

MONACO 5 METZ 0
Ligue 1, February 11, 2017
World-class strikers can finish with both feet and Mbappé showed he was in that elite category with a stunning left-footed effort against Metz. He got the ball on the edge of the box and before the defence could react, he effortlessly stroked the ball home with the inside of his weaker foot.

MONACO 7 RENNES 0
Coupe de La ligue, December 14, 2016
The teenager bagged a hat-trick against Rennes in this League Cup clash and the best of his brilliant treble was his first. Collecting the ball just inside the opposition half, Mbappé left the defence for dead with his blistering pace, sprinted into the box and beat goalkeeper Paul Nardi with a cool, curling finish.

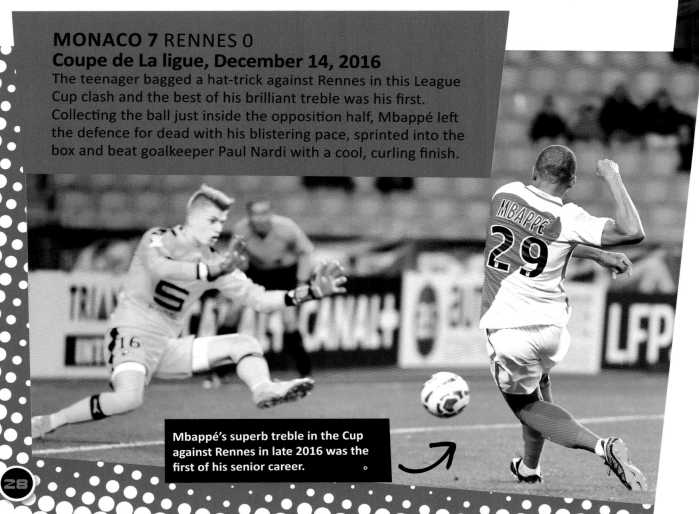

Mbappé's superb treble in the Cup against Rennes in late 2016 was the first of his senior career.

The striker's header in the league against Montpellier highlighted his natural ability to find space in the box.

MONACO 6 MONTPELLIER 2
Ligue 1, October 21, 2016

Mbappé might not be the tallest player but his towering leap against Montpellier for his first goal of the 2016–17 season proved he's deadly in the air. He ghosted in behind the defender and rose to perfectly meet a curling right-wing cross, heading the ball past the diving Geoffrey Jourdren into the bottom corner.

MONACO 4 NANTES 0
Ligue 1, March 5, 2017

Fast reactions are crucial for a top-class striker and Mbappé showcased his remarkable speed of thought with this goal. The ball unexpectedly took a deflection off a Nantes defender and in the blink of an eye he had found the back of the net with a beautiful, right-footed volley over his shoulder.

Great players have great reactions and Mbappé proved that with this brilliant instinctive finish for Monaco against Nantes.

Mbappé has scaled the heights in the professional game thanks to his relentless training regime and search for football perfection.

TRAINING WITH MBAPPÉ

The PSG star is an amazing natural talent but has only reached the pinnacle of the game with hard work and dedication on the training ground.

Ever since he was a youngster growing up in Paris, Mbappé has put in the hours in training to improve his skills to become the world-class player he is today. Even though he's already a World Cup winner and three-time Ligue 1 champion, he still works as hard as ever in practice as he does during a match.

His brilliant attitude and professionalism was obvious to everyone at his first senior club Monaco. "He breathes football, sleeps football, actually nothing else is on his mind," said the club's vice-president Vadim Vasilyev. "He didn't even go out when we won the title in 2017. He is really dedicated and has a very competitive spirit. He wants to break all the records.

"He reminds me a bit of Cristiano Ronaldo, because I also know him well. Kylian knows all the records and he always wants to be the youngest

Mbappé continues to train hard in order to realise his dream of becoming the best player in the world.

Brazil legend Pelé is a big fan of the PSG star and believes the youngster can win multiple World Cups with France.

player on the pitch to score, the youngest player to win this cup, to win the title. He's a truly great competitor."

Mbappé always takes training as seriously as playing. At the start of the 2018–19 season he decided to keep count of the number of goals he scored in training with PSG and in February 2019, just days after he netted against Manchester United at Old Trafford in the Champions League, he had already reached 100. To mark the milestone his team-mates presented him a T-shirt reading

"Mbappé 100 Training" on it.

The first famous footballer to keep a tally of his number of goals in training was Brazil legend Pelé and the three-time World Cup winner believes the Frenchman's work ethic and talent to become the greatest player on the planet.

"He won the World Cup at the age of 19 and I did it when I was 17 years old," he said. "I teased him saying he had almost equalled what I did, but I think he can become the new Pelé and I don't say that as a joke."

MBAPPÉ IN NUMBERS

Here are some key stats that tell the story of the incredible career of the PSG superstar.

Mbappé has achieved incredible things for club and country in his first five seasons in the professional ranks.

16 Age at which he made his professional debut for Monaco against Caen in Ligue 1 in December 2015.

39 Number of goals scored in 43 appearances for PSG in all competitions in the 2018–19 season.

180,000,000 Transfer fee in euros Paris Saint-Germain paid Monaco to sign the teenager in summer 2017.

3 Number of Ligue 1 hat-tricks he scored for PSG in 2018–19.

25 Distance, in yards, of his wonder strike for France against Croatia in the 2018 FIFA World Cup final.

534 Minutes Mbappé played for France at the 2018 World Cup in Russia.

7
Shirt number given to Mbappé by PSG ahead of the start of the 2018–19 season after his World Cup heroics.

4
Number of times Mbappé has won the Ligue 1 Player of the Month award.

34
Minutes it took Mbappé to score on his Champions League debut for PSG against Celtic in September 2017.

62
Days after his 17th birthday when he scored the first goal of his professional career, netting in the league against Troyes in February 2016.

87
Number of goals scored for Monaco and PSG in all competitions as at August 1, 2019.

13
Number of international goals scored for France in his first 33 appearances for his country.

MBAPPÉ'S SUPERSTAR TEAM-MATES

The World Cup winner is surrounded by world-class players at PSG. Here are some of his legendary team-mates.

Mbappé and Neymar shared an amazing 111 goals in all competitions in their first two seasons together in Paris.

8 mai 2018

THIAGO SILVA

Silva is a hugely experienced central defender who began his professional career in his native Brazil back in 2004. Signed from Italian giants AC Milan in 2012, Silva was quickly named captain and led PSG to the 2103 Ligue 1 title, ending the club's 19-year wait to be crowned French champions. Under Silva's superb leadership, PSG have won 15 major trophies and he has been in the Ligue 1 Team of the Year in all of his seven seasons.

NEYMAR

The outrageously talented Brazilian playmaker became the most expensive footballer in history when he signed for PSG from Barcelona for €222 million in August 2017. A Champions League and La Liga winner with the Spanish giants, Neymar scored more than 50 goals in his first two seasons at PSG and was named the 2017–18 Ligue 1 Player of the Year after helping PSG wrap up a famous league and cup treble.

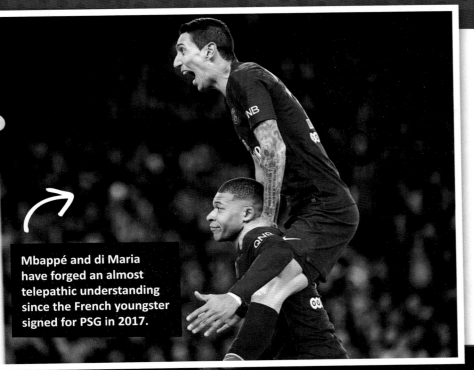

Mbappé and di Maria have forged an almost telepathic understanding since the French youngster signed for PSG in 2017.

ÁNGEL DI MARÍA

An elegant, intelligent Argentinean left-footed midfielder, Di María joined PSG from Manchester United in 2015. He reached 100 caps for his country in 2019 and has won league titles in Portugal with Benfica and in Spain with Real Madrid, as well as three Ligue 1 crowns with PSG. He won a Beijing 2008 Olympic Games gold medal and played in the 2014 World Cup final.

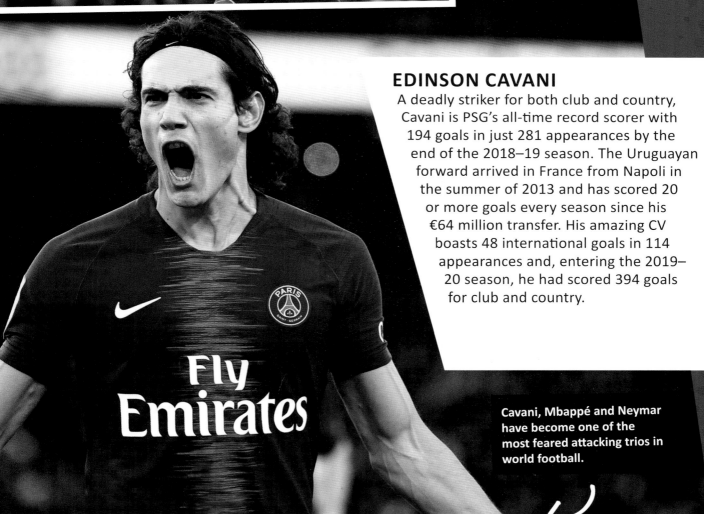

EDINSON CAVANI

A deadly striker for both club and country, Cavani is PSG's all-time record scorer with 194 goals in just 281 appearances by the end of the 2018–19 season. The Uruguayan forward arrived in France from Napoli in the summer of 2013 and has scored 20 or more goals every season since his €64 million transfer. His amazing CV boasts 48 international goals in 114 appearances and, entering the 2019–20 season, he had scored 394 goals for club and country.

Cavani, Mbappé and Neymar have become one of the most feared attacking trios in world football.

GLOBAL STAR

After his incredible performances for PSG and France, Mbappé has become one of the famous and popular players on the planet.

Fame follows success and after inspiring France to victory in the 2018 World Cup, Mbappé suddenly found himself in huge demand from both fans and the media. The new face of French football was everywhere and just three months after the final he appeared on the cover of famous American magazine *Time*.

He was only the fourth footballer, after Lionel Messi, Neymar and Mario Balotelli, to grace the cover. "His breath-taking soccer skills have propelled him to global fame in a matter of months," wrote the reporter who interviewed him.

"He earns more money than he could ever have imagined. Nike is designing pricey sneakers in his name. LeBron James wants to see him when he comes to town later that week. And when he steps out on the street, people beg him for autographs." The magazine also named Mbappé as one of the world's 25 most influential teenagers.

To celebrate France's triumph a giant, 11-storey billboard was fixed to the side of an apartment block in Bondy, near Paris – where Mbappé grew up – showing the local hero with his thumbs up. The message was "*Bondy: Ville des possibles*", which translates as "Bondy: Town of possibilities".

He is also a big star on social media and has more than 35 million followers on Instagram. That's more than both former US President Barack Obama and current French President Emmanuel Macron. His official Twitter account has over three million followers.

Mbappé is also very popular in Cameroon, because of his father's African heritage and during the World Cup, football fans chanted his name on the streets. One landlord in the city of Douala even renamed his bar "Mbappé" during the tournament in tribute to him.

His fame continues to grow and on PSG's preseason tour of Asia in 2019, he was honoured with a cartoon of his trademark goal celebration drawn by a famous Japanese manga cartoonist.

THE MAN.
THE BASICS.

BULK HOMME
THE BASIC MEN'S SKIN CARE

After his exploits at the 2018 World Cup, Mbappé has been in huge demand with some of the world's biggest and most exclusive brands.

With millions of social media followers worldwide, his fan base and popularity has grown rapidly in recent years.

Mbappé is now a global sporting icon but he still remains a hero in his childhood Paris suburb of Bondy.

BONDY VILLE DES POSSIBLES

Fly Emirates

PLAYING FOR PSG

After less than two full seasons in the Monaco first team, Mbappé was heading back to his home city to sign for big-spending Paris Saint-Germain.

It came as no surprise, after his achievements during the 2016–17 season, that bigger and richer clubs than Monaco would try to lure their star player away and, in August 2017, PSG made their move for Mbappé with a staggering €180 million offer.

The teenager was keen to return Paris and, despite having two years left on his Monaco contract, he was on his way to the French capital. The deal made him the most expensive teenager in football history, and second most costly player, behind new team-mate Neymar. The fee was the biggest agreed between two clubs in the same league.

"It is with great joy and pride that I join Paris Saint-Germain," he said. "For any young person from the Paris region, it is often a dream to wear the red and blue jersey and experience the unique atmosphere of the Parc des Princes.

"I really wanted to be a part of the club's project, which is one of the most ambitious in Europe. Alongside my new team-mates, I intend to continue my progression while helping the team achieve the very big objectives it has set itself."

Handed the number 29 shirt, Mbappé joined PSG initially on a year-long loan with an option to make the deal permanent after his first season with the club.

Mbappé's record-breaking move to PSG in the summer of 2017 was the next step in the teenager's incredible professional progress.

"It is essential for French football that we keep and help develop such a great talent in our championship," said PSG president Nasser Al-Khelaifi. "Among players of his age, he is without doubt the most promising in the world due to his immense technical, physical and mental qualities. Since his emergence at the highest level, he has earned an excellent reputation as a young talent who is very respectful, open, ambitious and already very mature."

PSG president Nasser Al-Khelaifi was prepared to break the bank to lure Mbappé away from Monaco and back to Paris.

Mbappé's new home ground is the Parc des Princes, which has a 47,929 capacity and was opened in 1972.

ICI C'EST PARIS

WINNING THE TREBLE

Mbappé enjoyed a sensational debut season in Paris as PSG claimed a clean sweep of the domestic silverware on offer in France.

Some big-money signings fail to justify their price tag, but Mbappé was not one of them as the teenager quickly proved he was the real deal at PSG, forming a deadly attacking trio with Uruguayan Edinson Cavani and Brazil's Neymar.

He helped himself to his first Ligue 1 goal against Metz in early September and never looked back, opening his European account for the club, just four days later, in a 5-0 thrashing of Celtic in Glasgow in the UEFA Champions League. His first PSG double came in early November, against Angers.

Victory for Mbappé and PSG over Les Herbiers in the final of the Coupe de France completed a famous treble for the club.

His first trophy came in March when PSG faced Monaco in the final of the Coupe de Ligue (League Cup) in Bordeaux. Mbappé didn't score against his old club, but won the penalty, scored by Cavani, for the opener and set up Ángel di María for the second, as PSG romped to a 3-0 win and a fifth successive victory in the competition.

He did not have to wait long for more silverware. PSG headed south to face Monaco in April, knowing victory would give them the league title. Although Mbappé missed the game with an injury, his team-mates got the job done without him with a stunning 7-1 win. For the second consecutive season, Mbappé was part of a championship-winning team.

The final piece of the jigsaw was the Coupe de France. Mbappé scored four goals in four appearances to send PSG into the final, where they met third-division minnows Les Herbiers at the Stade de France. The youngster hit a post and had a goal ruled out by VAR, but it didn't matter as PSG ran out 2-0 winners to complete the treble.

In total, Mbappé scored 13 goals in 27 appearances in the season. For the second year running he was voted Ligue 1 Young Player of the Year and also was selected for the Ligue 1 Team of the Year, rounding off a stunning debut season in Paris.

Winning Ligue 1 in 2017-18 in his first season with PSG was the second successive French title of Mbappé's short career.

Mbappé won the Coupe de Ligue for the first time in 2018 after PSG despatched his old club Monaco in the final in Bordeaux.

COUPE DE LA LIGUE

A COACH'S DREAM

What Mbappé's coaches and managers say about the PSG and France superstar.

"Kylian is unbelievably talented and he is a very positive person too. I can say that he is very hungry to score goals and to win games. Even in training, he is very competitive and he has that special skill to give the other players a positive mindset and to get them to improve their game. These are the things that make him unique. And it's just great that he is playing for our team. You can feel that the people welcome him in every stadium here in France."
Thomas Tuchel, PSG manager 2018–present

France boss and World Cup winner Didier Deschamps handed Mbappé his international debut against Luxembourg in March 2017.

"Kylian is able to do extraordinary things. Look at his stats. He is efficient. Look at the goals he scored with his club and with us. He also made assists. He is an offensive leader for PSG and for us as well. Kylian always adjusts himself to our needs. We know he has the quality."
Didier Deschamps, France manager 2012–present

"Mbappé is not surprising me at all. I've seen him work every day since he was 17 and it was obvious. We know that he's a player of great quality with a spectacular future ahead of him. If he maintains this level and this evolution, he can be the successor of Cristiano Ronaldo."
Leonardo Jardim, Monaco manager 2014–18

Mbappé spent the first two seasons of his professional career under the watchful eye of Monaco manager Leonardo Jardim.

"He wants to be a great player and he is going to grow up into that role. Kylian is progressing well. He has great talent and great desire. The idea when we signed him was that he would help the team grow, and the team would help him grow too."
Unai Emery, PSG manager 2016–18

"The first time I coached him was when he was six years old. You could tell he was different. Kylian could do much more than the other children. His dribbling was already fantastic and he was much faster than the others. He was the best player I've ever seen. In Paris, there are many talents but I'd never seen a talent like him."
Antonio Riccardi, AS Bondy youth team coach

Unai Emery was the coach who welcomed Mbappé to PSG and helped him mature into the one of the game's most exciting and consistent performers.

WORLD CUP HERO

Just over a year after making his international debut for *Les Bleus*, Mbappé headed to Russia in the summer of 2018 to play for France in the FIFA World Cup.

Mbappé wasn't born when France were crowned world champions for the first time in 1998 and he had never played in a senior tournament when he touched down in Russia, 20 years later, to spearhead his country's bid for a second title.

He was named in the line-up for the first group game against Australia, won 2-1 by France, but it was in his second appearance, against Peru five days later, that Mbappé hit the headlines, grabbing the only goal with an instinctive tap-in to seal three priceless points. At 19 years and 164 days, Mbappé became France's youngest-ever World Cup finals goalscorer.

A goalless draw with Denmark was enough to send *Les Bleus* into the knockout stages, where they faced Argentina. The round of 16 match was a classic, and Mbappé was the difference between the two teams, winning a penalty after a brilliant run from inside his own half for France's first goal before scoring two second-half goals as France won 4-3 to earn a place in the quarter-finals.

His first goal was a clinical 64th-minute, left-footed finish after a magical dribble in the box. Four minutes later, he scored his second with a thumping right-footed strike from the edge of the area that beat keeper Franco Armani at the far post. His double made him only the second teenager in World Cup history, after the legendary Pelé in 1958, to score twice in a World Cup knock-out match.

Les Bleus had no trouble beating Uruguay in the quarter-finals, running out 2-0 winners, but Belgium were tougher opposition in Saint Petersburg. Despite another dazzling performance from Mbappé, a second-half header from defender Samuel Umtiti decided the semi-final tie.

France were through to the final and Mbappé was on the verge of the greatest moment of his career.

Mbappé's first ever goal in the World Cup finals came against Peru in the Central Stadium in Ekaterinburg.

The Frenchman was in devastating form for France in the side's 4-3 thriller against Argentina in the last 16.

MOSCOW FAIRYTALE

The 2018 World Cup final saw France face Croatia in the Russian capital and Mbappé produced a superstar performance as *Les Bleus* lifted the famous trophy.

Mbappé was just 19 years and 207 days old when he ran out on the pitch at the Luzhniki Stadium on July 15, 2018. He was just the third teenager ever to play in a World Cup final but if he was suffering any nerves, he didn't show them.

A crowd of 78,000 in the stadium – and billions more on television around the world – watched the match, which exploded into life in the 18th minute when France took the lead thanks to a Mario Mandžukić own goal. It was 2-1 to *Les Bleus* at half-time and the stage was set for Mbappé to make his mark.

His first game-changing contribution came in the 59th minute when he burst into the box from the right wing and cut the ball back for Paul Pogba to score. Six minutes later, he got his own name on the scoresheet, rifling home a stunning low drive past Danijel Subašić from outside the area that made it 4-1 to France. The final finished 4-2 to *Les Bleus* and five months short of his 20th birthday, Mbappé could call himself a world champion.

"I am very happy," he said after the game. "I spoke about my ambitions before the World Cup. The road was long but it was worth it. We're proud to have made the French happy, that was our role.

"Becoming world champion sends a message. I want to do even better but winning the World Cup is already a good start. My goal gave us some breathing space. We worked hard all season and now it's time to celebrate this all summer long."

The teenager's four goals made him the joint second top scorer in the World Cup. He was also named the tournament's Best Young Player by FIFA and voted into the World Cup Dream Team, confirming the youngster's status as football's newest global superstar.

France lined-up for the 2018 World Cup final hoping to be crowned champions for the second time in the history of the tournament.

Mbappé's spectacular second-half strike in the final against Croatia was the pick of the six goals scored in Moscow.

France's 4-2 victory in the Luzhniki Stadium saw *Les Bleus* lift the World Cup trophy for the second time.

47

GOALS GALORE

PSG were head and shoulders above the rest in 2018–19, successfully defending their Ligue 1 title thanks to a flood of goals from Mbappé.

Mbappé's brace against Guingamp in August 2018 saw the star start the 2018-19 campaign with PSG in spectacular style.

Handed the No. 7 shirt for his second season in Paris, he enjoyed the campaign of his young career. Mbappé scored a double in his first Ligue 1 game against Guingamp, and was on 10 goals after only eight appearances in all competitions.

In October, he scored an incredible four goals in the space of 13 minutes at home against Olympique Lyonnais. It was the first time in 45 seasons that a teenager had scored four times in a French league match.

By the end of November, Mbappé had already netted 11 times in the league and in December he became the first winner of the Kopa Trophy, awarded by *France Football* magazine to the best Under-21 player in the world.

The second half of the 2018–19 campaign saw him register two Ligue 1 hat-tricks – the first against Guingamp in January and the second against his old club Monaco in April. In March, the second goal of a double against Caen at Stade

PSG successfully defended the Ligue 1 title thanks to Mbappé's best-ever season in front of goal.

The inaugural Kopa Trophy was Mbappé's individual reward for his prolific form in 2018.

Michel d'Ornano took Mbappé to 50 career goals for PSG.

The treble against Monaco came just hours after PSG had been confirmed as league champions for the sixth time in seven seasons, this after nearest challengers Lille had failed to beat Toulouse to keep the title race alive.

PSG eventually took the title by 16 points. They lost their final match – 3-1 away to Reims – but Mbappé's second-half strike was historic, as PSG became the first Ligue 1 club ever to score in all 38 of their league matches in a season.

Mbappé's contribution to the club's triumph was stunning. He was PSG's leading scorer with 33 goals in only 29 league appearances. It also made him Ligue 1's top striker, earning him the Golden Boot, and he was voted the league's Player of the Year for the first time.

GREAT PSG GOALS

Kylian Mbappé has been deadly in front of goal since his record-breaking move to PSG. Here are five of his most spectacular strikes.

ANGERS 0 **PSG 5**
Ligue 1, November 4, 2017

The second goal of Mbappé's Ligue 1 brace against Angers showcased his incredible talent, pace and balance. Collecting a difficult bouncing ball, he controlled it with his first touch, glided effortlessly around keeper Mathieu Michel and finished with his left foot.

BAYERN MUNICH 3 **PSG 1**
Champions League, December 5, 2017

Anticipation is a key part of Mbappé's game and his speed of thought was on show when he netted against German giants Bayern Munich. Finding enough space in the penalty area to get on the end of a chipped pass, he scored with a glancing header into the far corner.

Scoring against European heavyweights Bayern Munich aged just 18 only enhanced the teenager's reputation.

Rated the number one keeper in the world, David de Gea was still powerless to stop Mbappé netting at Old Trafford.

PSG 2 LILLE 1
Ligue 1, November 2, 2018
Great strikers score from both short- and long-range and Mbappé showed he could produce from outside the box with a stunning goal against Lille. Sprinting in behind the back four, he received the ball 25 yards out and, after just one touch, produced an amazing shot that curled into the top corner.

MANCHESTER UNITED 0 PSG 2
Champions League, February 12, 2019
Mbappé lit up Old Trafford with a fantastic goal that sealed a famous win for the French side. Racing into the area, the forward somehow found the space between two United defenders, latching onto a low cross from the left before netting with a deft flick that gave keeper David De Gea no chance.

An audacious chip in the opening game of the campaign led to a flood of goals for Mbappé in 2018–19.

GUINGAMP 1 PSG 3
Ligue 1, August 18, 2018
Mbappé's first game of the 2018–19 season saw him bag a brace for PSG and his second goal was a work of art. Picking up possession outside the box, he ghosted into the penalty area in space between two defenders before beating the onrushing Karl-Johan Johnsson with a brilliant scoop.

RECORD BREAKER

Despite only turning 20 in 2018, Mbappé has already set many records for both club and country in his incredible career.

Mbappé became Monaco's youngest goalscorer, setting the record with his strike against Troyes in February 2016 aged 17 years and 62 days.

His transfer fee of €180 million from Monaco to PSG in August 2017 made him the most expensive teenager in football history.

His four-goal display for PSG in their 7-0 demolition of Lyon in October 2018 equalled the club record for most goals scored in a match.

Mbappé became France's youngest World Cup finals goalscorer, aged 19 years and 183 days, when netting the winner against Peru in Ekaterinburg on June 21, 2018.

In 2017, Mbappé became the first PSG player to win the Golden Boy trophy as the best Under-21 player in Europe.

At the age of 16 years and 347 days, the teenager became Monaco's youngest ever player when he made his debut for the club against Caen on December 2, 2015. He broke the previous record set by Thierry Henry back in 1994.

His goal for PSG against Bayern Munich in December 2017 was his 10th in the UEFA Champions League. At 18 years and 350 days, he became the youngest player in the history of the competition to reach double figures.

Thierry Henry had held the record as Monaco's youngest ever player until Mbappé's debut in late 2015.

On February 22, 2019, Mbappé, aged 20 years and 64 days, grabbed a double against Nîmes to become the youngest player in Ligue 1 history to net 50 goals.

Mbappé succeeded PSG team-mate Neymar as the Ligue 1 Player of the Year in 2019.

When the teenager scored twice for Monaco against Nantes in March 2017, he became the youngest player for 30 years to reach 10 goals in a Ligue 1 season.

In 2018–19, Mbappé became the youngest ever PSG player to win the Ligue 1 Player of the Year award. His 33 goals also made him youngest PSG player to win the Ligue 1 Golden Boot.

EN ROUTE TO EURO 2020

After starring at the 2018 FIFA World Cup in Russia, Mbappé returned to the international stage the following year to spearhead France's attempt to win the European Championship.

Les Bleus were crowned kings of Europe for the first time back in 1984. They won the trophy for the second time in 2000 and with Mbappé now established in the team, hopes are high that they can complete a hat-trick of titles.

France began their qualification campaign in March 2019 with an away game against Moldova. The visitors stormed into a 3-0 lead, but the home side got one back late on, only for Mbappé to kill off any hopes of a fightback with a brilliant strike from the edge of the box that completely deceived the keeper to seal a 4-1 win.

Three days later, he was on target again when Iceland were defeated 4-0 in Paris. His devastating pace took him between the two central defenders and, after picking up possession from an Antoine Griezmann pass, he somehow managed to keep his balance and score from close range for his 12th international goal.

The next round of matches were in June and Mbappé didn't score in *Les Bleus'* 2-0 victory on the road against Turkey, but he did make it three goals in four appearances in qualifying when France faced the minnows of Andorra.

France cruised to a comfortable 4-1 win against Moldova at the tiny Zimbru Stadium in Chişinău.

It took him just 11 minutes to break the deadlock. *Les Bleus* broke at speed from their own half and Mbappé was away, once again latching onto a through ball from Griezmann before leaving a desperate defender in his wake with an unstoppable burst of pace. Goalkeeper Josep Gomes came sliding out, but Mbappé calmly converted with an outrageous chip. France maintained their 100 percent record in qualifying with a 4-0 victory.

Tougher tests will follow for France to reach the UEFA EURO 2020 finals but with Mbappé in such hot form in front of goal, the current world champions will fear no one.

Mbappé's strike against Iceland in the Stade de France was his second successive goal in Euro 2020 qualifying.

The striker's sublime finish against Andorra in June 2019 helped ensure France made it four wins in four.

MBAPPÉ'S HONOURS & AWARDS

All you need to know about the career of football's new global superstar.

In 2017 he received the Golden Boy award – given to the Under-21 player considered to have the most potential by top European football journalists.

His stunning displays as a 17- and 18-year-old in 2016–17 earned him a place in the UEFA Champions League Team of the Season alongside Cristiano Ronaldo and Lionel Messi.

The teenager scored six goals in the 2016–17 Champions League campaign to fire Monaco into the semi-finals.

He has won four French Professional Players' Association Player of the Month awards – in April 2017, March and August 2018 and February 2019.

At the end of all of his three full seasons he has made the Ligue 1 Team of the Year, with Monaco in 2016–17 and at PSG in 2017–18 and 2018–19.

Mbappé's first major award came in 2016 when he was included in the UEFA Team of the Tournament after the European Under-19 Championships in Germany.

Mbappé's 2016–17 Ligue 1 Young Player of the Year award was the first of a hat-trick of wins for the France star.

Mbappé was named the Ligue 1 Young Player of the Year three times in a row, 2017–19. He was also voted the Player of the Year at the end of the 2018–19 season.

After starring in the *Les Bleus*' World Cup win in 2018, Mbappé was named the French Player of the Year by *France Football* magazine. It's an award legends such as Thierry Henry, Zinedine Zidane, N'Golo Kanté and Franck Ribéry have won in recent years.

Mbappé was included in the FIFA FIFPro World XI for the first time in September 2018, one of three French players alongside N'Golo Kanté and Raphaël Varane. Mbappé also made the World XI in 2019.

Russia President Vladimir Putin was on hand to present Mbappé with his FIFA Best Young Player award at the 2018 World Cup.

Mbappé earned the FIFA Best Young Player Award after the 2018 FIFA World Cup, emulating team-mate Paul Pogba who won the award four years earlier in Brazil. The teenager was also named in the FIFA World Cup Dream Team at the end of the 2018 tournament.

WHAT NEXT FOR MBAPPÉ?

The best is yet to come from the dazzling French star for both club and country.

Few footballers have made such a massive impact on the game at such a young age and there's no doubt that Mbappé will only improve as a player as he gains in experience. The big question is which club will he be playing for in the future.

His current deal with PSG runs until the summer of 2022 but, after two sensational seasons in Paris, it's no secret that some of Europe's biggest clubs are desperate to lure him away from France. Real Madrid, Manchester City and Liverpool have all been linked with him and although PSG insist they don't want to sell, the rumours about his future won't go away.

When Madrid unveiled new signing Eden Hazard in June 2019, in front of 50,000 fans at the Bernabeu stadium, some sections of the crowd could be heard chanting: "We want Mbappé, we want Mbappé." Liverpool manager Jürgen Klopp has been tracking the youngster since his breakthrough 2016–17 season with Monaco, while he's still in touch with former Monaco team-mates Bernardo Silva and Benjamin Mendy, both now playing for Manchester City.

Mbappé himself has dropped hints that his future might not be in Paris. In May 2019 he picked up the Ligue 1 Player of the Year award and after collecting his trophy told reporters that he it was not guaranteed he would play for PSG for the next three seasons of his contract.

"It's a very important moment for me," he told the media. "I come to a turning point in my career. I have discovered a lot here, and I feel it is maybe the moment to have more responsibility. I hope that it can perhaps be at Paris Saint-Germain – that would be a great pleasure. Or, it maybe elsewhere with a new project."

Whether Mbappé decides to pursue a "new project" remains to be seen, but what is certain is that the Frenchman is already set to be arguably the best player of his generation.

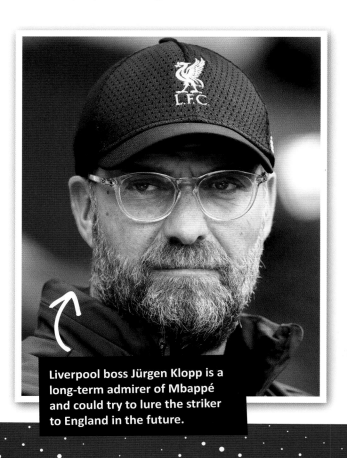

Liverpool boss Jürgen Klopp is a long-term admirer of Mbappé and could try to lure the striker to England in the future.

Mbappé is already a PSG legend but the star admits he is unsure how long he will stay in France.

Mbappé and France team-mate Benjamin Mendy played together at Monaco and could be reunited at Manchester City.

QUIZ TIME

Here are 20 questions to test how much you really know about the PSG and France superstar. All the answers can be found in the preceding pages of this book.

1 What was the name of the suburb in Paris where Mbappé grew up?

2 The youngster had posters of which football star on his bedroom wall?

3 His mother played which sport professionally?

4 At the age of 11, Mbappé went for a trial at which Premier League club?

5 Against French club did the forward score the first goal of his professional career in February 2016?

6 How many goals did he score for France in the UEFA European Under-19 Championships in 2016?

7 What did Mbappé do for the first time against Manchester City in February 2017?

8 Against which country did he make his international debut in March 2017?

9 He scored his first international goal in August 2017 against which team?

10 How old was Mbappé when he became the youngest French player to score in a World Cup finals fixture against Peru in Ekaterinburg in 2018?

11 Against which country did he score a World Cup double in the knockout stages of the World Cup?

12 What was the score between France and Croatia in the World Cup final?

13 What individual award did he win after France's World Cup victory?

14 What was his transfer fee (in euros) when he signed for PSG from Monaco in 2018?

15 How many goals did he score in PSG's 7-0 thumping of Lyon in October 2018?

16 Which magazine named Mbappé the French Player of the Year at the end of 2018?

17 What shirt number was Mbappé given by PSG ahead of the 2018–19 season?

18 Against which club did he score the 50th league goal of his career in February 2019?

19 How many goals did the striker score for PSG in all competitions in 2018–19?

20 How many times has Mbappé won the Ligue 1 title?

The UEFA European Under-19 Championships in 2016 was the first major international tournament of Mbappé's career.

Mbappé was the second top scorer in the UEFA European Under-19 Championships in Germany in 2016.

Mbappé was just 18 years old when he won his first cap for France from the bench in a 2018 World Cup qualifier.

The youngster was sensational for *Les Bleus* in their famous victory over Croatia in the 2018 World Cup final in Moscow.

PICTURE QUIZ

Kylian Mbappé is rapidly becoming accustomed to winning major prizes. Can you spot which trophies he's holding in these pictures? The answers are on the opposite page.

A

B

C

D